Palewell Press

The Scen

From Libya, London and every world I live in

Farrah Fray

Palewell Press

migrations

The Scent Of My Skin–From Libya, London and every world I live in

Published by Palewell Press Ltd
http://www.palewellpress.co.uk/

First Edition

ISBN 978-1-911587-02-6

A CIP catalogue record for this title is available from the British Library.

Palewell Press Ltd supports the Forest Stewardship Council® (FSC®) the leading international forest-certification organisation. Our books carrying the FSC® label are printed on FSC®-certified paper. Their printing and binding complies with ISO 14001 (Environmental Management) and 50001 (Energy Management).

Dedication

This book is dedicated to my wonderful father (may god bless his soul). I love you.

Acknowledgements

I would like to Camilla Reeve for this opportunity, and for her constant support and guidance along the way. You have made one of my biggest dreams come true. I remember walking across Strand and jumping in joy in after our first meeting. I would also like to thank Mary Powell for taking an interest and showing Camilla some of my poems, as well as Caroline Summers for believing in me right from the very start when we were only acquainted co-workers discussing our hobbies. I am also incredibly fortunate and blessed to have wonderful friends. A special thanks to my best friend Marwa Fichera for her unwavering love and support throughout our friendship and this book, and to my close friend Ahmed Drebika for always offering his time and thoughts. I am grateful for both friendships. I am also very grateful for a strong connection with Muneat **Mahfud**, the cover designer and artist, who has been through thick and thin with me; from an international school in Libya in 2010 to the heart of London, 2017–sitting together and talking about our shared dreams; some of which are manifested through this book. I would also like to thank Ayah Al Wahedi for her encouragement and belief in both myself and this book. Jump, and the net will appear, right?

Contents

Section 1: Foot-traffic herbs

Noun: Foot-traffic herbs are those with kitchen-worthy, foot-tolerant foliage. If mowed, they come back tender, plush and attractive. Best of all is Creeping oregano (Organum vulgare "Humile") that forms a dense, traffic-tolerant mat less than three inches high.

Triangle

The
shape
of fingers
st re tch ed
at a crossroad
with the lining, of
your clothes, lines that
were going to be perpendicular
but chose to lean forward a little bit
more, legs, bedsheets, corners that became
unknown angles, the outline of your tongue a stencil
fingers, latticed - a thousand small triangles, the spaces
between the pages of an opened book bound together by
excitement
bent knees
and the spaces
in   between
the broken daughters of diamonds
looking for their other
half.

South of the river

It had already made me nostalgic
long before I met you
the market on a warm summer's day
the worst and best customer experience
you could ever pay
cheap for,
memories of being younger,
uncomfortably warm
running up pavements and rolling down hills
sweaty,

-Happy-

After that night, memories stopped
belonging
to categories
or time.
And after a while they became petals
that offered an expiry date for pain;
I left them on the floor
with a young girl, I once knew
south of the river.

Yours

Cliché is a shared form of art and
I am
yours-
yours across the seven seas
yours in the deft desert breeze
yours in the roots of the coldest trees
yours when you've long forgotten me

Yours when perfume fills Sunday eve
in every nimble kiss and hastened tea
yours when I've crossed the seven seas
when I've long since left the gallery

yours when my ashes are the only thing
remaining, yours is the sorrow I would always bring.

I couldn't want you anyway

I couldn't want you anyway.
getting out of bed became too monumental a task, too much a
feat.
I was tired from visiting the places where your hands slid up my
thighs and you weren't there.

You had left months ago
but I asked everyone why you stopped caring

and some words would remind me of you.
In fact, all words would remind me of you.

Even the time passing by
would remind me of you
no matter how quietly it cut through

and that warm sickly pain
quickly renewed
when you told me you were seeing someone new.

And this didn't mean we couldn't keep in touch
and your words, your words, your words they just—
crashed into each other and stared at me
like children falling
through a scary dream,
like the pavements gave way to this pitiless heat
and I was a blistering joint of meat

like the weight
of the heartbreak
sank its teeth
and clutched onto life so frantically

and ate and ate and ate and ate
and in a drunken stupor would regurgitate
and scream and whine about how it tasted like
shit—

I would think about you
and what you whisper to her
opposite you in the euphoric blur
and perhaps
she has
freckles that twitch
when she smiles

and legs that can
outrun you
for miles and miles

and perhaps
she just
says the right things
at the right time

and her words
come out
less jumbled
than mine

and perhaps
you are kissing
her as I speak
so
I couldn't want you, anyway.

Spring

I rinsed out stories of us
over and over again
until their colours slunk away,
tossed them into wells
on vacations
only to pull them back out.

In the greyness of the city without you
I imagined you sitting next to me
your glossy veins in between my hands,
our fingertips eclipsing the sun.

I didn't know what to make of
rain that pelted from every direction,
streets full of men who looked like you,
coffee cups held by cold hands,

longing for something
that had already gone.

Dahlia

You were beautiful.
You wore cranberry lipstick
and laughed a lot,
your skin was uninhabited by worries
and stress.
Barren of the landmarks of battles fought
it invited me quietly.
I never met you,
but I know
that scars have healed,
that you have fought the same battle as me
and it might have taken you years to laugh so freely,
but here you are,
and I know
I shouldn't envy you
but I do.

Trauma

My English teacher used to say
that when trauma happens,
sometimes
your brain just keeps replaying it

Having just returned from Libya,
I understood what he meant
but it confused me that
I also replayed memories of you
in the morning,
wondering if you were
eating shakshouka,
or smoking a blunt.

And before the grass got goose bumps
I sat on the front steps of a church,
wondering
if you were ever going to call me back.

My English teacher would probably say
I should be happy you never did.

Flowers

your smell
like asphalt
won't wash off
in the shower

the rain
like your fingers
fall onto my lap
as flowers

the phone
like a flower
longs to be picked

from the grip
of the soil's womb
be ripped

the soil - like my skin
longs to be kissed

instead I must watch
flowers touch your lips.

Autumn

I am holding tightly a cup of tea
As if it were your body's heat
I am willing
the brown carpets and the fragrant
Kitchen tops I grew up climbing on

To make everything seem
Like this is how things should be

I go for walks when it's rainy and dark
Glad that there isn't a specific park
That reminds me of you

And yet

There is nowhere else I'd rather be
Than with your hands over me
My boots in your room
under your books

grappling with your hands
And your smile
And you.

Books

Under the sun sparkling fruit flies debated their existence
in such a crowded city;
I wondered if they knew about John Donne,
if like me, words could add to their worth
amongst waxy 1970s adolescents smoking on the stairs,
their slender legs and chipped nails
the most elusive statement about themselves

My body canvassed against cigarette stubs and Spring
mottled with salvaged memories,
a sweaty lust to be anyone else,
in the most beautiful building I've ever seen
I wish I'd taken one last picture of you
followed the echoes of our embrace

I wish I was unafraid of myself
without a care or memory to trace.

Bridges

The year drifted by
Grey mornings were spent looking
out of the windows of lecture rooms
across the bridge
and the spaces in between
people's legs
wondering if love grew there

I watched Eden in the afternoon
her roots and her veins and her hair drunkenly stumbling

short circuiting across London's streets
waiting for you to grab her watery waist
with muscles that never tired
from thinking of you

realizing why hearts don't get tired of beating

the earth from spinning,

my eyes from looking across the bridge

Trying to forget the things you did.

Section 2: Milk

Noun: Milk - an opaque white fluid rich in fat and protein, secreted by female mammals for the nourishment of their young;
Verb: To milk – to exploit or defraud by taking small amounts of money over a period of time;
Adjective: Milk-white, used to symbolise feminine purity.

Wedding

I think of my beautiful cousin
his ivory cheeks dimpling, laughing.
I imagine him at my wedding
all that makeup on my face -
the inevitable fountain of red lipstick,
his confusion at the bloodshed and
women telling me what to do,
being unable to play cards on the patio
or drink tea while lying down
or tell my husband to fuck off
and cook his own goddamn pasta.
I think of unopened kitchen doors,
the wisdom of children,
and the ugliness of my beautiful mother
laughing, twinkling, dancing.
I hope she cries on my wedding night.

Wedding vows

1) Promise
To be kind, listen
When I tell a story
And my body exhales

2) If you find yourself washing the dishes
That it is not a startling discovery
If the smell of
Fairy liquid and hot water escapes
Like strawberry shisha from a limp body
On a rainy night in Edgware Road

3) Promise that it will remind you not
Of things that your mother might say

4) That the sunset will remind you
Of the shades of pink that my skin can lay
Or

5) Summer

6) Bank holiday weekends

7) Who my favourite artist is

8) A fridge full of cider

Or

9) Forever.

Meche

Meche –
strategically placed strands skipping over
to the other side of the colour spectrum,
wrapped around bronze fingers
under a tangerine sky
but stripped of warmth,
they cascade onto women's naked bodies
when hair is untied,
rope weathered enough
to be undone.

Note - Meche is a form of highlighting hair that was a popular trend and style in the USA and Europe in the early 2000s-and remains very popular in Libya as well as many other countries in the Middle East. It entails bleaching strands of hair until they are varying shades of very light blonde. Besides the breakage and damage this creates, and many other hair trends have similar effects; the specific importance of this trend to Libyans is they believe it automatically makes you more beautiful, as it is synonymous with being fair which is also seen as a symbol of beauty. At weddings, it is essential for a woman and she often gets pressured into it if she doesn't want to. But most of the time they are docile or brainwashed enough to do it. As most Libyan women have very very dark hair, the process can often be long and tedious, but in the name of pleasing men and other women it is considered worth doing.

Patience

Patience is a virtue
and we are taught to become great
at waiting
because good things come to those who wait
heaven, and angels and pearly gates
and childhood friends, playing by a lake

but angels already have their circle of friends
and days don't ever really end
patience waits
in between your thighs
and good things

come

all the time.

Rallying Cry

To stand upright is the best way to stand,
feet burrowed firmly in the summer sand

If you don't like farms, or cooking meals
a refund will be issued before breaking the seal

And if you hate children they won't look at you twice
women are measured by their ability to divide

Though his hands might be too rough for you
you've just got to sleep it through

And though you might cry from the pain of his girth
nothing is harder than proving your worth

And should you want to have a job and see Berlin
you're the very woman they will not let in

But if you are sensually easy at being someone else
that is the hallmark of a golden girl

Intelligence is an asset if it challenges Freud,
to speak of the past and be placidly void

You must be skilled in handling rifles
but tender enough to let yourself be stifled

to pull the trigger on yourself instead of him
and feel absolved of committing any sin.

Ambition

she should softly
pad down the stairs

be softly aroused
by morning prayer

her hips, untouched
should rise and fall

before his hills
the sun should be small

tender, fair
muted like brie

soupy air
in summer's heat

she should

accommodate, curl,
taste –
sweet

consist of many
empty seats

and if she has a bouncing baby boy
she should encourage him to destroy

toss his plates
anywhere

always have something
to declare

when he's old enough
he can bludgeon more rooms

inside another woman's womb.

Women

I know women with terracotta veins
and curly hair that reveals the shape of the wind
who like other women want to please men

And they do, by unravelling their hair
and lightening their skin
avoiding the sun,

And trying to avoid sin
Roses and Barbie, their fervid dreams
of legs that collapse like melted cream
and sandcastles built to be wet and dry
for children to squeeze, their father to pry

away

May I know women who refuse to be repressed
women with curls that tumble over their breasts

who mop the verandas with their dry feet
and ask for fries, and something sweet

And may I know men who refuse to accept
when power is given by those who are oppressed.

Boys don't think like us

Boys don't think like us,
it's just the way the world dictates –
Arabic kohl comes from a very anguished place
like comedy, and poetry, and every art
and one of them is clutching at my heart
as tears stream down her Bambi eyes
as she seeks for answers across her thighs

In between strategically placed lashes
which swing like jammed doors
and shooting stars and windy shores
and things that fly up into the sky
and adamantly refuse to expire
like confusion
and Disney films
and Crayola pens

Like the yawning stretch of land
between now and then
Like emptiness
that I tell her is because
Boys
don't
think like us.

Rust

His love for me was

Rust

Her lips were as red as her
hair

I scoffed

We might have liked the same
makeup;

Or not

She was Icelandic, I was Mediterranean

I think

Her bio seems impressive

I blink

I might place

I drink

My hands on top
of hers

I un think

(Hold her hair behind the sink)

I might realise
we have more in common

I sink

I might find out where she works

I weigh

Listen to her sing
I stay

Under her breath

I'd pray

She would be beautiful
I'd say

And I would understand

His way.

War

She was taken away from her favourite place
Her family had arranged a date
in late July, under the summer sky

Thighs not against the cool bar of a bus stop seat
but rather
shivering under a heaving breeze

Washed over by the waves of his faltering knees
Buildings will topple over each other
the way he topples over her

Like the towers in Leptis Magna
abandoned by men,
he will demand she clean up his mess

The way men do when they wage war
against countries stronger than them
believe that she is now worthless in her ruin

That no one will visit her but him
when she smiled despite his thrust,
was sombre in the face of lust,

He didn't know that
landmarks are both beautiful and strong
in their ruins, welcomed by everyone.

Section 3: Coffee

Noun: Coffee - a hot drink made from the roasted and ground bean-like seeds of a tropical shrub. Introduced to the world in the late 16th century: the word comes from Turkish kahveh, from Arabic qahwa, probably via Dutch koffie, bitter-sweet.

Warning

Warning, Caution: keep away
plastered on the forehead of a 20-tonne truck
on a superhighway in a city that made strong people
run out of luck

I read the veins on his neck and they said x marks the spot

Warning: rain forecast
Hurled rain was nothing
It was sparkling Spring that took away clothes
left Zeus shivering in his boots

Warning: 40% vol
Warnings that were never felt but rather read,
thinking good god, I wish I was dead
killed by the soft shake of his legs

Warning:
It's not the truck that will kill you
It's everything else.

Mocha part 1

I met you in a coffee shop

The outline of my lips
on a coffee cup
smiling back at me
faltering somewhere between wet and dry
like the slant of your cheeks that narrowly avoid the rain outside

Your laugh was alien to me
The distance between us
a bent arm

Behind your body the rain danced restlessly,
walking looked like flying,
legs turned into wings
flew over puddles that were nests asking to be abandoned

The sun didn't need to come back around
Winter beat summer and you beat the sun to my heart
Ah, ah, we sighed.

Mocha part 2

I met you in a coffee shop
It felt like we'd known each other for years

The next night you told me secrets that dug graves in my body,
fragments of sentences I revisited in moonlight

Like, you love fucking in the outdoors under starry skies
in the middle of a hot summer

It made you really hard to make a woman orgasm with your lips
and your most favourite place to kiss

was
her neck or ears
closely followed by
an inner thigh

I saw the glitter that fell from her eyes
all the variations of soft splitting sighs

The way your tongues tinkled like glasses of white wine
in between listless hands that dangled restlessly
like the canopies of beds in different cities

I wanted to visit every city and every coffee shop with you
and remember our first conversation

And then I remembered that you maybe always talk
to women in coffee shops

There are so many places you could be right now –
One of them in another woman's trembling arms

I stopped going to coffee shops.

My favourite colours

I told you to stop talking about fucking

And you asked what my favourite colour was
as if it mattered;
you wanted to grope my breasts,
leave powder-blue dimples on my back,
dig your fingers into the coffee-coloured hollows
of my collarbones,
breathe onto the opaline cambers of my shoulders,
tear open my chest and pull me closer,
multiply red continents on my warm skin,
divide the number of fingerprints.

You wanted to paint a rainbow on a canvas
the colour of the desert.
It made me sad not knowing what my favourite colour is.
There are so many I could choose from.

The first day you left

The first day that you left
I hadn't slept for three whole nights.
The first coffee spun cartwheels,
pavements multiplied.

The first day that you left
I learned warmth wasn't from the sun,
it came from your body
and I knew clothes had to be

souvenirs of places I would never see again
knew without knowing I had secrets and fears
and quivering oceans of frightened tears.
The first day that you left I realised time freezes,

life doesn't go on, but waveringly retreats.
The first day that you left
I remembered I forgot to choose.
How could this day go on without you?

Girl combat, London

Vulnerable girls –
help prevent them from becoming
caught up and
protect them
from becoming deaf,
losing the rhythm
and taste of sentences
as well as sex

Teach them that words are a martial art
that can be used to say no
as well as yes,
help them visit their tombstones
and accept
their ghosts
without pulling the trigger

Some girls are weapons,
lengthy jail sentences,
projects,
waiting to be funded
others
buried, six feet under.

Comment section

We wore
comfortable trainers,
reassuringly balmy jumpers that
consented to covering every crevice
We were
always on the run from something good
even on days we were too tired to wake up,
let alone choose something smart to wear

We were
Enraptured, we showered
half asleep to bathe in the bay at the core of each plastic chair.
Once a week,
we were allowed to be helplessly in love with the premise
things are not as good as we'd expected
we had run out of emotions to feel,
and words to say
to make things better
But I guess we wanted them to be
because we talked about them.

Battersea Park Road

I saw a man from the window of a coffee shop
on Battersea Park Road
He was wearing a red poncho and a red hat.
He didn't seem to care, or maybe he couldn't.
Made me wonder why I care what colour clothes I wear.
I didn't know if he was coming or going
Made me realise I never really knew if people
were coming or going
or leaving this very earth in a few minutes
or seconds or tonight
even if it looked like they were coming,
walking, dancing, kissing.

He staggered, gently.
I don't know if people stagger quickly or slowly
but it reminded me of staggering deadlines
and how when you write
you have to stagger,
only look at the steps
in
      front
          of
               you
instead of the whole mountain.

Maybe that's what he was doing.
He didn't look at the end of the road.
I'm not sure if he even knew (or cared) where it ended
But he got there eventually
and maybe he was more alive than I had ever been.
He made me question a lot of things.

Healing

Today
I am healing
I dance in the kitchen
I dance with my eyes

Today,
the world is worth dancing for
I go to parties
and I talk to the girl crying outside

Sometimes I am the girl crying outside
and some nights I think that I'll die
but today
I am healing.

Section 4: Sugar

Noun: Sugar - a sweet crystalline substance obtained from various plants, especially sugar cane and sugar beet, consisting essentially of sucrose, and used as a sweetener in food and drink;
Verb: To sugar or sugarcoat something - to talk about or describe it in a way that makes it seem more pleasant or acceptable than it really is.

You

And so, I dived headfirst into the deep blue sea
of false and worthless memories

How could you compare me to a drunken kiss,
childhood teachers you would never miss,

an awkward conversation that will not devolve,
notes on the fridge that's struggling to hold

limp, stale picnic treats?

How bitter it feels being remembered as sweet.

Sweet

I didn't peel off the pillowed seams of wounds
limping closer and closer to the truth
and swallow all flavours of hurt –
recoiling alive, breathing

dying –
only
for you

to call me sweet
for trying.

Unwritten Hopes

I hope I run into you full blast head on head over heels
in the middle of a book shop

I hope it's cold outside that we get
coffee that I'd be wearing a skirt and
knee high boots

that you grab my legs and I sit on your lap
and we reclaim winter over and over again

I hope I run into you head on and we turn into sparks and flames
that destroy cities

I hope we destroy cities and have kids that destroy
what's left of our tired brains

I hope I run into you head on like a car crash and we fly into the
stars and swallow the universe
the way it swallowed us

I hope we create as much pain as we have been given and enjoy
our lives together,
forever.

Cinnamon

The closest thing to ginger, the most puzzling brown
at war with east and west in her curls and her frown,
olive branches nettled under Libyan sun
her eyes were the colour of Pepsi and rum.
His kiss etched gingerly on the slopes of her skin,
her bargain with God—elusive like cinnamon.

Serenity

Talking to him was
orange blossom, the season of
lukewarm thick sahlab, fervidly swilled down
like fleeting dreams
between waking and sleep

a resolution reached
the excitement and calm of wanting
to jump onto the sofa and smile

under it all,
a woman slowly taking her clothes off
again
hoping
that it would always be the season.

Sometimes

Sometimes he's sleeping softly
and other times
he wakes up
in the back seat
of my mind
and reminds me of

everything.

Daydream

Whenever I'd see an airplane I used to wish I was up there
in one of the seats in beige tights and heels,
drinking cold coffee
laced with artificial air and anticipation.
On the other side, somewhere, you'd be waiting for me
like in a film,
we'd stagger home and order takeaway,
sleep together. You'd tell me secrets from the past
and we'd rifle through truth and memory.
I remember you liked lying down when it was sunny,
it never materialised, needless to say
but I always enjoy looking up at airplanes.

Karina

Your name reminds me of
tambourines ringing in a music lesson

a beautiful hotel in Libya, Corinthia
Port in Arabic, a crowded 'Mena'

small hands lifting a pan lid in the cucina

I wished you were a childhood friend
braving P.E lessons, walking on the beach with me,

growing accustomed to the sound of whistling,
the bitterness of peaches, heat of the sun

settling for Miranda instead of coke and rum;
and watching things get so far gone—

but I'm glad it's only the letters in your name
that dance to the melody

of the country,
of the language that breaks promises.

Ayah

We had the best sandwiches, right?
The funniest jokes, trips,
I never liked picnics until I met you,
dreaded international school
more than hellfire,
I was hella younger,
I felt sad a lot of the time
caught up in myself.
But together we were the loudest,
the brightest.
Like staggering drunks,
we jumped on the steps and skipped every class,
hid behind pillars,
ran exceptionally fast.
High on liquid courage,
the water sprayed by sprinklers,
Monkey bars,
terrible teachers,
terribly funny teachers,
like us,
just figuring things out,
having a good time
and a picnic.
When I remember how we were back then,
I fall in love with Libya again.
We had the best sandwiches, right?

Marwa

The truth feels warmer when I'm sitting opposite you.
You give me advice even when you don't want to,
when we've long rinsed the topic through and through,
pushing away some Sunday blues,
but you were honest, you made it clear
I could do better, stretch my arms towards the sky,
collect the twirling seconds in a call duration
like the numbers on your oven door on New Year's Day
when we were laughing about the cheesecake that we'd burnt.
Numbers that didn't matter because
there was little to discern,
lost seconds, months, minutes wondering
how different things would be if I hadn't met you;
if the Muscovado cheesecake at the coffee court wasn't so
overpriced
and Clapham was north of the river;
if my uni bar had no view
and Libyans didn't need a coup;
if we could cross the border with the same walk and the same
talk
of a best friend of a best friend of a battle fought;
but if the universe was bigger and less cruel
I still wouldn't want a life without you
and if I find myself in a departure lounge
thinking about Sunday blues,
my last meal will be cheesecake,
my last phone call to you.

Section 5: Footpaths

Noun: Footpaths - paths created for people to walk on. Most popular in the countryside, they can also be found in forests, on mountain ridges and in busy cities. Most commonly made for people walking to school, work or church, some footpaths were also made for pilgrimages.

Airports

Uncovering the veil of nostalgia,
being torn off on the runway
on cold plastic seats
in slumbering spring,
food that tastes like old memories,
a baby crying and another asleep,
people all walking towards one thing

The struggle of remembering a battle always fought
in the waiting rooms of grey glass airports,
coming face to face with the past,
her heavily kohled eyes
crying at last.

Freeways

I spent hot summer nights
bargaining with Hades to bring him back,
journeys between Libya and Tunisia
wishing he was the one driving,
that we were all going down a freeway
away
that he would comment on the sunrise,
like he always did
one hand out the window
when we were only kids,
his eyes in the mirror a more heavenly sight,
gleaming, smiling, turning on the lights.
I hold my sister's hand in bed
and we try to pretend
that the lights are still on,
that the sunrise is right in front of us,
that
Hades exists.

Father

It's hard to describe missing someone

The emptiness of a walk down a one-way road,
cuts that only you could sew,
the sound of your laugh, low and bright,
the excitement of twinkling night headlights,
salt and pepper hair, softly curled,
the limitlessness of your arms unfurled,
the realisation that nothing would ever smell
the way that they did before farewell,
that I will always long for nights unspent
drinking tea and inhaling incense,
I long for the world and the birds and your smile,
a waltz in unadulterated freestyle,
the giddy sway of lilies of the Nile
and for you to visit, if once in awhile.

To come bounding in the doorway,
to meet you there,
to laugh with you about everything, anywhere,
to be younger, less troubled, lighter than air.

To pick me up and take me with you,
show me, chuckling, thousandth-floor views
but unfulfilled desire sank into infinitude,
the misery
in missing you.

Half of

Dear,

I thought
of all the words we didn't say
and haven't said to each other yet

all the words in the universe
that tumbled like sweat

I thought of all the stars
and the clichés people spoke of
and noted how I wanted
to give them to you
sprinkle them like confetti
in the living room

and it made me sad
to think of the colours that exist
pink sunsets, blue Mondays
that we missed

volcanic summers, frightened falls
that rose and fell without us all

or the time I dropped our little
sister down the stairs
and no other hurt
could ever compare

the time our dad
played Diana Ross
and never showed
that he was lost

bumpy rides
on speedy freeways
sweltering heat
that simmered for days

memories that I held
without you here
fights that lasted
years and years

timid jokes
I was afraid to tell,
an unwavering belief
in magic spells

and if you find yourself
angry at me
I can give you all
these memories.

Libya

The cold sweat
lingering
on my Pepsi can

Our names written
on the sweet soft sand

The wind
would fold
and unfold
and fold
like
the stories
my grandma told

Brown leather seats
were hot to touch
and hot to hold
and hot to clutch

Hot to speak
and
hot to breathe,
my sister would squeal
excitedly

We had
to open
the windows
wide
and start conversation
about
all our
lies

And next thing
you
know
and
you know
and y'know,

Politics
was
the overthrow
the warmest cloak
my midnight robe

And the night
fell too soon
for us
to
cope.

Tunisia

Tunisia was a country that wanted to make use of every square
metre;
fields of chilli, petrol sold by the ten litres

in opaque blue gallons;

I loved the tenacity in laying her clothes bare
seducing the tourists who simply loved to stare

making mosaics that made you remember
something you didn't see
grape vines and flowers scattered carelessly
taxis that would take you to the infinite skies
held by rhythmic talk and tapestries of white lies,
sandy streets that grappled with palm trees
she short breath of air before a sneeze-

And she yawned and stretched all day long
her hips dancing to a Tunisian song

Tunisia was a country that wanted to make use of every square
metre,
unlike her neighbour, people didn't defeat her.

Lost children

"We want go to London"
they whispered relentlessly,
those words written
in the same staccato
as their hot footsteps

Uneven surfaces, like the curls of their hair
were unable to refract light,
the sun, a concave lens
that watched everything but gave
nothing

They thought that wind
blistering through their crumbling streets
would be gentler where there was no heat
like the breeze that sweeps through your room,
2 am on a summer morning

And films where they hug in the snow and go to restaurants
on a broken TV
in their city,
walls were emblems of victory

Rain, heavenly beads of relief
London a distant, jazzy dream
and
"We want go to London,"

they kept saying.

Found Immigrants

For two days
they saw death in between their eyes -
mermaids gasping for air.
Only one of them lived.
He knew how to swim.

Travel

Capri pants, softly humming,
the novelty of bare feet on a sandy beach,
people propelled
by their culture and not their jobs -
selling, buying
eyeing
up tourists,
holding onto narrow mountain ridges
and running down lobby stairs like kids.
At nightfall that gave way to loud laughter

but for some, they didn't remember childhood,
nightfall gave way to shortfall
and whispering,
Will it be like this forever?
Before falling asleep
descending into unmoving heaps
in a forest, somewhere
like toys thrown to the side of the room
their fate dependant on fickle mood
suspended across different altitudes
from mountains that screamed, 'we don't want you'-

They were not travellers, but refugees.

English Weather

My mother is exceptionally good at cooking
cutting vegetables without chopping boards
or recipes

You will notice her kohled eyes pointing
in the direction of food and conversation
and deft, slender wrists that also watch and listen
with eyes of their own

Those same eyes will rifle through children's books and
teacher's comments
in between departure lounges, grey pavements,
to hover over women's thighs
weaving in and out of crowds,
and on top of lovers, rooted in the grass

You will notice her by the dandelions
wishing she was back in her hometown.
You will also notice me wishing she would
pack her bags and leave me behind

Cold, warm, wet
like English weather.

Train stations

9:37 am
I thought about the road less travelled
about flinging myself onto it
just to touch someone
to feel anything but this feeling
If walls could speak maybe
They would have hurriedly told me how many embraces they
saw
or how many you had after me.
Maybe maths, facts
would become my friends
instead of unwritten messages which challenged statistics
which probably weren't true -
Literature that could have meant anything
you wanted it to
and left me wondering if I ever knew
anything.
How could you define death?
The grey ravine beyond the yellow line,
slow steady quiet breaths,
little letters on a long page,
the b-b-beat of my heart,
and all its synonyms,
blow, stroke, flicker, flutter, jerk, tremble
gone.

Where do I go?

Where do I go?
I sleep in libraries

Between book shelves
and wet windows

I see London, sprawled
on every route

Every landmark impaled
by you

Fingerprints that you left
on her body

Fleeting moments shorter than a
drop of rain

A city
that refuses to forget;

Wrestling with her past and
raining -

where do I go?

Where do I go?

SAQF

I remember my brother used to climb onto the roof
whenever the satellite wasn't working.
My mother would wait until she was completely sure,
afraid to waste his time
but he found it fun, loved to climb.
Sometimes my cousins would hold the ladder for him,
other times he liked feeling the wall against his skin.

Her face would shift between laughter and horror as she
watched
but he'd always make her laugh,
the way charming boys do

One day our neighbour's son was hit by a stray bullet.
He had climbed over the grapevines to watch a wedding.
And my mother had a hard time saying that it would have been
better if he fell,
or if there was no wedding at all
or that no one picked fruits anyway.

But his mother still watered the grapes
and spoke about his eyes, which were the colour of dates
under the sun,
would answer every stray text
or better still, joke with other women about death.

Farrah Fray - Biography

Farrah Fray is a native Libyan born in London. Her work explores culture, displacement, and feminism. She is influenced by both London and Libya as well as travels and people.

Palewell Press

Palewell Press is an independent publisher handling poetry, fiction and non-fiction with a focus on human rights, social history, and the environment. The Editor may be reached via enquiries@palewellpress.co.uk